MiNi MaKeRs

mini
SCIENCE FUN

by Rebecca Felix

Lerner Publications / Minneapolis

Lerner Publications Company
A division of Lerner Publishing Group, Inc.
241 First Avenue North
Minneapolis, MN 55401 USA

For reading levels and more information, look up this title at www.lernerbooks.com.

Main body text set in Bembo STD 16/25.
Typeface provided by Monotype Typography.

Library of Congress Cataloging-in-Publication Data

Names: Felix, Rebecca, 1984- author.
Title: Mini science fun / by Rebecca Felix.
Description: Minneapolis : Lerner Publications, [2016] | Series: Mini makers | Audience: Ages 7-11. | Audience: Grades 4 to 6. | Includes bibliographical references and index.
Identifiers: LCCN 2016018653 (print) | LCCN 2016020018 (ebook) | ISBN 9781512426342 (lb : alk. paper) | ISBN 9781512428124 (eb pdf)
Subjects: LCSH: Science–Experiments–Juvenile literature. | Miniature craft–Juvenile literature. | CYAC: Handicraft.
Classification: LCC Q164 .F354 2016 (print) | LCC Q164 (ebook) | DDC 507.8–dc23

LC record available at https://lccn.loc.gov/2016018653

Manufactured in the United States of America
1-41385-23326-8/4/2016

Photo Acknowledgements
The images in this book are used with the permission of: © Mighty Media, Inc., pp. 4, 5, 8 (left), 8 (right), 9 (top), 10, 11 (top), 11 (middle), 11 (bottom), 12, 13 (top), 13 (middle), 13 (bottom), 14, 15 (top), 15 (middle), 15 (bottom), 16, 17 (top), 17 (middle), 17 (bottom), 18, 19 (top), 19 (middle), 19 (bottom), 20, 21 (top), 21 (middle), 21 (bottom), 22, 23 (top) 23 (middle), 23 (bottom), 24, 25 (top), 25 (middle), 25 (bottom), 26, 27 (top), 27 (middle), 27 (bottom), 28 (top), 28 (bottom), 29; © Sean MacD/Shutterstock Images, p. 4 (food coloring); © pelfophoto/Shutterstock Images, p. 4 (paintbrush); © Rob Marmion/Shutterstock Images, p. 5 (top); © hanakaz/Shutterstock Images, p. 5 (beads); © photka/Shutterstock Images, p. 5 (paint); © Nipaporn Panyacharoen/Shutterstock Images, p. 6 (moss); © olias32/Shutterstock Images, p. 6 (seaweed); © Rawpixel.com/Shutterstock Images, p. 7; © bscmediallc/Shutterstock Images, p. 8 (glitter); © George Dolgikh/Shutterstock Images, p. 8 (goggles); © studiovin/Shutterstock Images, p. 9 (batteries); © ZaZa Studio/Shutterstock Images, p. 9 (graph paper); © Coprid/Shutterstock Images, p. 9 (scissors); © Chad Zuber/Shutterstock Images, 9 (seaweed); © vipman/Shutterstock Images, p. 9 (test tubes); © Anastasia_Panait/Shutterstock Images, p. 12 (glitter); © Aleksander Erin/Shutterstock Images, pp. 14 (red paintbrush), 16 (paint); © Marques/Shutterstock Images, p. 18 (markers).

Front cover: © Mighty Media, Inc.

Back cover: © Mighty Media, Inc. (left, right); © kemalbas/iStockphoto (buttons); © Vladvm/Shutterstock Images (scissors).

CONTENTS

Getting Started 4

Before You Begin 6

Teeny Volcano Eruption 10

Tiny Tornado 12

Small Submarine 14

Little Science Lab 16

Wee Water Cycle 18

Teeny-Weeny Walking Water Drops 20

Mini Ecosystem 22

Itsy-Bitsy Button Race Car 24

Miniature Merry-Go-Round 26

Wrapping Up 30

Glossary 31

Further Information 31

Index 32

Getting Started
SMALL SCIENCE

Have you ever participated in a science fair? You've probably studied science at school. Or maybe you've watched a science program on TV. Even if you haven't, cool science is all around us! Everything we can see and touch is made up of elements. Biology is at work in your backyard garden and your family pet. And you experience meteorology every time you look out the window. There's so much science to discover!

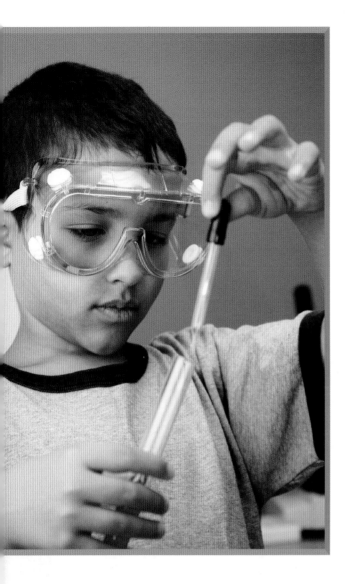

With so much science all around us, it can be hard to know where to start experimenting. But what if you could explore science on a smaller scale? Imagine creating a twirling tornado that can fit in your hand. Picture perfecting a wee race car that flies down a tiny ramp. Mini science projects are fun to make and a great way to experiment. So gather your goggles, and get ready to explore science, one mini project at a time!

SLOW AND STEADY

Getting an experiment to work correctly can be tricky, even when the experiment is normal size. When materials and tools are small, science projects become even tougher. The key to creating super-small science projects is patience.

The first step to a successful science project is gathering your materials. You can find supplies for mini science projects at craft stores or hardware stores. An adult can also help you order supplies online. Before you start experimenting, make sure you have a clean workspace. Your work area should also be well lit. Tiny parts and pieces are easy to lose. If you're painting or using other messy materials, cover your work surface to protect it from spills. Most importantly, work slowly and carefully! Your science projects will turn out better if you take your time.

Work Safely!

Some crafts require the use of sharp tools and hot objects. That means they also require adult help. An adult will make sure your fingers, eyes, and workspace are protected as you craft amazing mini creations.

THINK
Like a Scientist

Scientists are always looking for ways to learn from and improve their experiments. As you craft and create your mini science projects, think about the science at work. What do you think is happening? Then **examine** your completed projects. What tools or techniques might bring about better results? What would you do differently next time?

Get inspired to learn more about the science concepts you encounter. Use your imagination to picture how your mini projects would work on a large scale. If you have questions, do some research. Experiment and craft small, but learn big!

TEENY VOLCANO ERUPTION

Create a **chemical compound** that will make a wee volcano explode!

MATERIALS

- clay
- tiny bottle
- disposable plate
- paint
- paintbrushes
- water
- 2 small cups
- spoon
- baking soda
- red and yellow food coloring
- vinegar

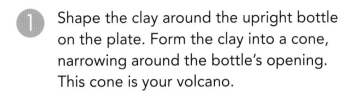

1. Shape the clay around the upright bottle on the plate. Form the clay into a cone, narrowing around the bottle's opening. This cone is your volcano.

2. Paint the volcano. Let it dry.

3. Fill a cup ¼ full with water. Add about half a spoonful of baking soda and a drop of red food coloring. Mix until the baking soda is dissolved.

4. Fill the other cup ¼ full with vinegar. Add in a few drops of yellow food coloring. Mix well.

5. Pour the red mixture into the volcano's opening. Fill the volcano bottle about halfway.

6. Fill the bottle the rest of the way with the yellow vinegar. Now watch the "lava" bubble and foam over the top of your very small volcano!

Tiny Science!

The amount of baking soda you need may vary, depending on how big your bottle is. If it is bigger than the one pictured, add a bit more baking soda. If it is smaller, add a bit less. Experiment until you have the right amount!

TINY TORNADO

Create a super-small, twisting storm inside a tiny container!

MATERIALS

- tiny bottle with tight-fitting lid
- water
- food coloring
- plate
- toothpick
- liquid dish soap
- glitter

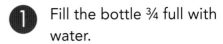

1 Fill the bottle ¾ full with water.

2 Put a drop of food coloring on a plate. Use a toothpick to add tiny amounts of food coloring to the water in the bottle. This will help you see the tornado.

3 Add a drop of dish soap to the jar.

4 Add a little bit of glitter to the jar. This will act as **debris** within the tornado.

5 Put the lid on tightly.

6 Shake or rotate the bottle. Hold it still, and watch for the tornado. Try rotating it in a different direction. Does anything change?

Tiny Tip!

As you shake the bottle, the water begins to spin. The water near the bottle's edges spins more quickly than the water near the bottle's center, creating a **vortex**. When you stop moving the bottle, the water near the bottle's edges slows down. The water near the bottle's center keeps spinning.

SMALL SUBMARINE

Discover what it takes to make a **miniscule** submarine stay underwater without sinking.

MATERIALS

- large, clear container
- water
- small watertight container
- small objects that will fit into the small container, such as paper clips, dice, small toys, and more
- paper
- pencil

1

2

1. Fill a large, clear container with water.

2. Gather together a wide variety of items that will fit into the small container. Choose some objects that are heavy and some that are light.

3. Fill the small container with items you think will allow it to stay underwater without completely sinking. Put the lid on. This will be your tiny submarine.

4. Place the small container in the large container. What happens? Does your submarine float or sink? Write down which objects are in the container.

5. Add and remove objects until the submarine hovers in the water.

6. Write down your findings. Were you surprised at what made the submarine hover?

4

Tiny Science!

Density causes objects to sink or float. Density is an object's mass divided by its volume. Objects that are less dense than water float. Objects that are denser than water sink. Some of the objects in your submarine are denser than water. But when you put them in the container, the volume of the container is great enough for your submarine to still float.

LITTLE SCIENCE LAB

Build a miniature science lab to store tiny equipment!

MATERIALS

- small box with lid, such as a cardboard jewelry box
- aluminum foil
- wooden craft sticks
- scissors
- all-purpose glue
- thin cardboard
- tape
- hole punch
- clear plastic tubing
- paper in several colors
- clear spray-bottle caps
- food coloring
- toothpicks
- markers
- wire

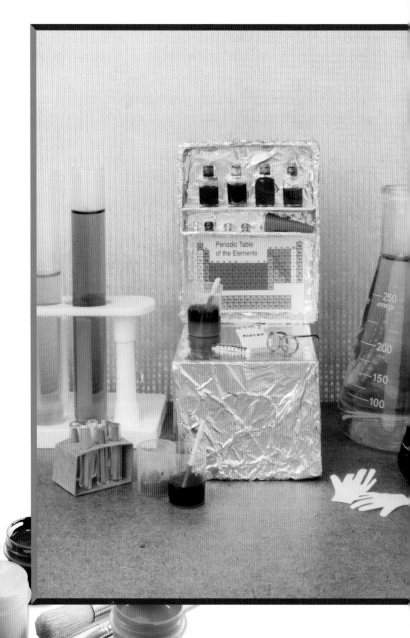

1. Cover the box and the lid with aluminum foil. Turn the box upside down.

2. Use wooden craft sticks to make shelves in the lid. Cut each stick so it will fit inside the box, and cover it with foil. Then glue the stick inside the lid.

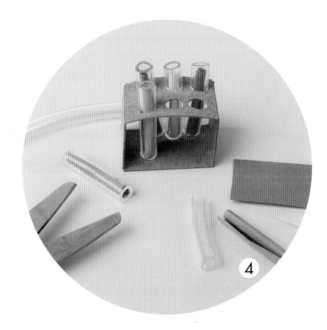

3. Put the lid on its end, and glue it to the top of the box.

4. Now make your mini lab equipment. Cut a strip of thin cardboard. Fold it into a cube, and tape along the seam. Punch six holes in the top of the cardboard. Cut plastic tubing to make the test tubes, and place them in the holes. Add a little piece of colored paper to each tube.

5. Fill clear spray-bottle caps with glue. Use a toothpick to mix in a few drops of food coloring. The caps will be beakers.

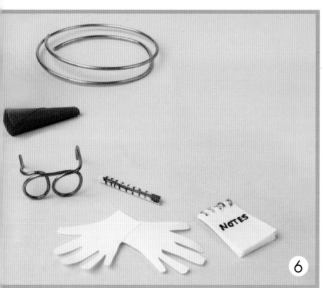

6. Cut a toothpick, and use markers to decorate it like a thermometer. Use paper, scissors, glue, and wire to create tiny gloves, glasses, a funnel, notebook, and more. What other tools might you want for your little lab? Use your imagination!

WEE WATER CYCLE

Create a tiny water cycle to understand how the world's water moves!

MATERIALS

- permanent markers
- small, zipper-close plastic bag
- water
- blue food coloring
- tape
- sunny window

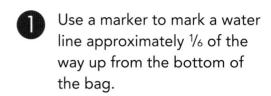

1. Use a marker to mark a water line approximately ⅙ of the way up from the bottom of the bag.

2. Draw a sun in one upper corner of the bag. Then draw a cloud in the other upper corner. Draw arrows going up toward the sun and down from the cloud.

3. Pour water in the bag up to the line you drew.

4. Add a drop of blue food coloring to the water.

5. Tape the bag to a sunny window. Now just sit back and watch your tiny water cycle work!

Tiny Science!

As the water warms in the sunlight, it starts to evaporate. The liquid water turns into a **vapor**. As the vapor cools, it forms tiny ice crystals and water droplets called condensation. These crystals and droplets attach to particles of dust and matter. This forms a cloud. When the cloud can't hold any more moisture, it releases the water as precipitation, such as rain or snow.

TEENY-WEENY WALKING WATER DROPS

Use the power of science to turn a simple string into a colorful craft supply!

MATERIALS

- 7 small, clear cups (medicine cups work well)
- water
- red, yellow, and blue food coloring
- cotton string
- ruler
- scissors

1. Fill four cups halfway with water.

2. Put two drops of red food coloring each in two of the cups. Put two drops of yellow in another cup, and put two drops of blue in the fourth cup.

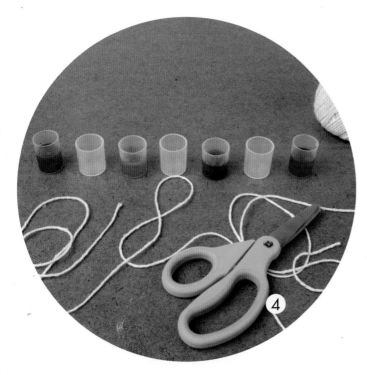

3. Line the cups up in this order: red, empty, yellow, empty, blue, empty, red.

4. Cut the string to about 20 inches (51 centimeters) long. Place one end of the string in the first red cup. Stretch the string over the cup's rim and into the next cup. Repeat until a portion of the string is resting in the bottom of all seven cups.

5. Now watch and wait. The water will travel from the full cups to the empty cups. Eventually, the water will be at the same level in all seven cups!

Tiny Tip!

When your experiment is complete, take out the string, and let it dry. Then use your colorful string to construct cool crafts inspired by science!

MINI ECOSYSTEM

Design a shrunken ecosystem perfect for **petite** creatures. Keep conditions right, and watch microscopic **organisms** thrive!

MATERIALS

- small, clear glass jar with tight-fitting lid
- tap water
- 3 containers with lids
- muck or sand
- aquatic plant
- water from a pond, creek, lake, or ocean
- spoon
- water conditioner
- tweezers

1. Wash out the jar with tap water. Do not use soap. Let the jar air dry.

2. Collect a bit of muck or sand from the bottom of a pond, creek, lake, or ocean. Put it in a container. Carefully dig up a small aquatic plant, including the roots. Put it in another container with some water. In the third container, collect some more water. Make sure the containers' lids are on tightly, and return home.

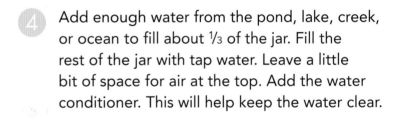

3. Scoop the muck or sand from the container to the bottom of the jar.

4. Add enough water from the pond, lake, creek, or ocean to fill about ⅓ of the jar. Fill the rest of the jar with tap water. Leave a little bit of space for air at the top. Add the water conditioner. This will help keep the water clear.

5. Use the tweezers to carefully place the aquatic plant in the jar. Bury any roots in the muck or sand. Keep the plant **submerged** in the water.

6. Close the lid tightly again. Check on the jar every day, and watch your mini ecosystem flourish!

ITSY-BITSY BUTTON RACE CAR

Watch physics at work with a wee race car that rides on button wheels!

MATERIALS

- newspaper
- small spring clothespin
- paint
- paintbrush
- scissors
- toothpicks
- 4 two-hole buttons of equal sizes
- all-purpose glue
- straw
- cardboard
- books

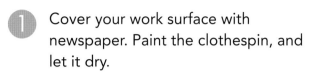

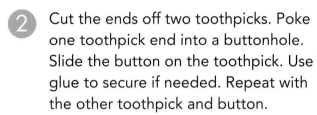

1. Cover your work surface with newspaper. Paint the clothespin, and let it dry.

2. Cut the ends off two toothpicks. Poke one toothpick end into a buttonhole. Slide the button on the toothpick. Use glue to secure if needed. Repeat with the other toothpick and button.

3. Cut off two pieces of a straw. Each should be about ½ as long as the cut toothpicks. Thread each straw piece onto each toothpick.

4. Poke each toothpick's open end through the open hole of a button. This makes two wheel sets. The buttons are the wheels, and the straw-covered toothpicks are the **axles**.

5. Clip one axle in the clothespin clip. Put a small dot of glue on the other axle. Glue the axle between the clothespin handles.

6. Make a ramp with a piece of cardboard. Use books to prop it up. Race your car down the ramp!

Tiny Tip!

Make several cars. Try button wheels of different sizes. Get a stopwatch and time your race cars on your ramp. Which cars went the fastest? Why do you think they were faster?

MINIATURE MERRY-GO-ROUND

Watch electricity and magnetism make a mini merry-go-round rotate!

MATERIALS

- pencil
- ruler
- thin cardboard
- scissors
- newspaper
- paint
- paintbrushes
- string

- 8 beads
- tape
- 4 ½-inch x ⅛-inch (1.3 cm x 0.3 cm) neodymium disc magnets
- AA battery

- 16-gauge copper wire
- wire cutter
- round-nosed pliers
- fine-point permanent marker
- cotton gloves

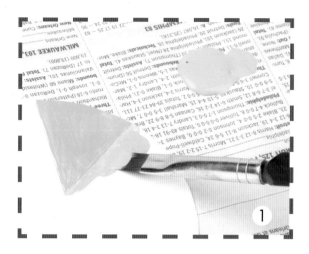

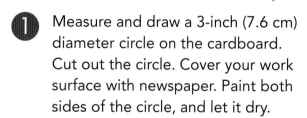

1. Measure and draw a 3-inch (7.6 cm) diameter circle on the cardboard. Cut out the circle. Cover your work surface with newspaper. Paint both sides of the circle, and let it dry.

2. Cut eight pieces of string, each 4 inches (10 cm) long.

3. Thread a bead onto each string. Tie a double knot at each string's end to keep the beads on the strings.

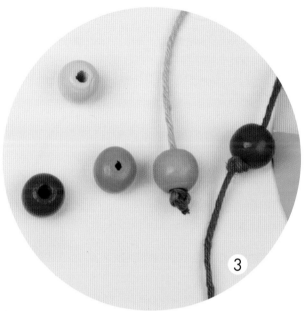

4. Tape the strings evenly around the underside of the cardboard circle. They should hang down about 2 inches (5 cm). Trim any **excess** string.

5. Stack the magnets on top of one another. Stack the negative end of the battery on top of the magnets.

6. Cut a piece of the copper wire 12 inches (30.5 cm) long.

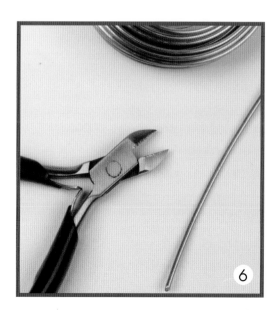

Miniature Merry-Go-Round continued next page

Tiny Tip!
Look for + and − signs on the battery to see which end is positive and which end is negative.

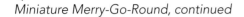

Miniature Merry-Go-Round, continued

7 Grip the center of the wire with a pliers. Bend the wire in half.

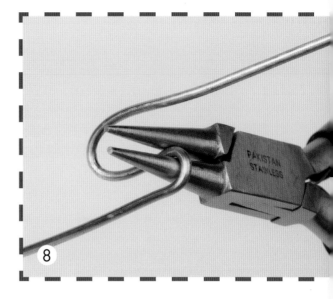

8 Move the pliers up ½ inch (1.3 cm) on one side of the center bend. Bend the wire the opposite way to form another bend. This should form a U shape in the center of the wire.

9 Bend the bottom end of the wire 2½ inches (6.4 cm) below the top bend. Your new bend should form an M shape.

10 Trim the excess wire so you have about 2½ inches (6.4 cm) on either side of the M. Curl the top ¾ inch (1.9 cm) of one end of the wire around the permanent marker. Repeat with the other wire end, curling in the same direction.

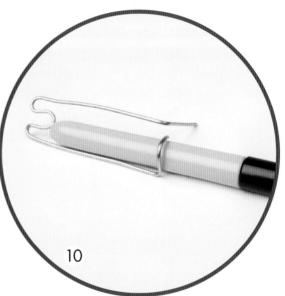

11 Put on the gloves. The battery will get hot! With an adult's help, balance the center bend on the positive end of the battery. The ends of the wire should be touching the magnets. When the wire is connected to the magnets and the positive end of the battery, the wire should spin. If it doesn't, adjust the wire and the magnets until you see the wire spin.

12 Make two small slits in the center of the cardboard circle to put the bent points of the wire through. Set the circle on the battery, and watch your miniature merry-go-round fly!

Show Off Your Science!

Finding neat ways to display your tiny science experiments is a big part of the fun! Put some popcorn next to your mini merry-go-round. This shows how small it really is! Think of unusual ways to display your other science crafts. Be creative, and have fun!

Wrapping Up
CLEANUP AND SAFEKEEPING

Cleaning up the laboratory is an important part of any science experiment. Be sure to put all of your supplies away. Keep track of tiny parts and pieces by storing them in small containers or plastic bags. That way they will be easy to find for future projects! Wipe down spills, and pick up leftover parts.

Find a safe place to display your science projects. Keep them out of reach of younger siblings and pets. Check on long-term projects, such as those with water or plant life.

Keep Crafting!

Get inspired by your small science projects. What did you learn from them? What would you do differently next time? What new scientific questions would you like to find answers to? Use these questions to create new miniature experiments. Think big and create small!

GLOSSARY

axles: the bars pairs of wheels turn on

chemical compound: a substance made of two or more elements that are chemically bonded

debris: bits and pieces of objects that are left behind

examine: to study something carefully

excess: extra or more than is needed

miniscule: so small, it is barely visible

organisms: living things

petite: small or trim

submerged: covered completely with water

vapor: very small drops or particles that hang in the air

vortex: a spinning mass of liquid or air that draws objects toward its center

Further Information

Cornell, Kari. *The Nitty-Gritty Gardening Book: Fun Projects for All Seasons.* Minneapolis: Millbrook Press, 2015.
Get your hands dirty and grow your own plants with these cool gardening projects.

Heinecke, Liz Lee. *Kitchen Science Lab for Kids: 52 Family Friendly Experiments from around the House.* Beverly, MA: Quarry Books, 2014.
Turn your house into a science lab with the fun projects in this book!

Science Experiments
http://www.funology.com/science-experiments
Check out the fun projects on this website, and think about how you could do them on a smaller scale.

Science Fair Projects
https://kids.usa.gov/science/science-fair-projects/index.shtml
Get ideas for your next science fair project at this website.

INDEX

biology, 4

cleaning up, 30

density, 15

displaying projects, 29, 30

ecosystem, 22–23

elements, 4

getting started, 4–9

materials, 6, 10, 12, 14, 16, 18, 20, 22, 24, 26, 30

merry-go-round, 26–28, 29

meteorology, 4

race car, 5, 24–25

safety, 7

science lab, 16–17

storage, 30

submarine, 14–15

tools, 6, 7, 8, 17

tornado, 5, 12–13

volcano, 10–11

walking water drops, 20–21

water cycle, 18–19

work area, 6, 7, 25, 27